NO HEART MORE TENDER

D0828019

NO HEART MORE TENDER

A book for the bereaved from a personal Christian perspective

by

Harry Read

Salvation Books
The Salvation Army International Headquarters
London, United Kingdom

All Bible quotations are from the
New International Version (*NIV*)
Copyright © 1973, 1978, 1984 by
International Bible Society
All rights reserved

All unattributed verse is by the author

Cover design artwork by Nathan Sigauke

SALVATION BOOKS

Published by Salvation Books
The Salvation Army International Headquarters
101 Queen Victoria Street, London EC4V 4EH
United Kingdom

Printed by UK Territory Print & Design Unit

CONTENTS

FOREWORD

Having known Harry Read for nearly 40 years, and being one of many recipients of his encouragement, friendship and kindness, I am honoured and pleased to welcome and recommend this most helpful volume.

We cannot think of Harry without also thinking of his beloved wife, Win. It is Harry's experience of life without her at his side that forms the loving basis for this insightful work.

Here is a book that combines tenderness and sensitivity with realism and practicality. My prayer, like that of the author, is that it will be used to help and to bless, to comfort and to encourage.

I record profound thanks to Commissioner Harry Read for all that these pages represent, not least the depth of his self-sharing and the tender sense, afforded to the reader, of Win and the life of deep faith shared with her.

Shaw Clifton
General

London, June 2010

PREFACE

In my devotions over many years I have kept a notebook near at hand to help me meditate and pray; an undemanding procedure that has proved its value over and over again. Quite early in this revised approach to prayer, and greatly to my blessing, I discovered that many of those thoughts and prayers came in verse form. It was almost predictable, therefore, that when my darling wife died, my bereavement experience should give rise to a number of poems and reflections expressing my feelings, my search for answers, and my faith.

There was no thought that any of this material would be made available for publication, but it has been suggested to me that these simple insights and inferences should be shared. How I wish experience had not qualified me to hold convictions on the subject!

If this small volume has any value it must be because it comes from within the experience of bereavement. The book is not the result of deductions made from thoughtful observations of the sorrows of others, valuable though such observations can be. Rather, the book is from a heart that has felt, and still feels, the catastrophic effects of loss; a heart that has struggled to reconcile the negative elements of grief with a tried and tested faith. Hopefully, these pages speak the language of the heart and will prove helpful to all who seek comfort and encouragement during their own days of almost overwhelming grief.

May it be so.

PROLOGUE

In bereavement we may often feel that the worst thing that could have happened to us has actually occurred. Our dreams, our most sanguine hopes have turned into the stuff of nightmares. We are bereaved. In consequence we feel fragile and vulnerable although a better description might be – we feel tender. Bereavement intensifies our tenderness but, in our tenderness, the overtones of weakness in the words 'fragile' and 'vulnerable' need not be present.

At first, the bewildering experience of bereavement may seem to challenge our faith in God and his providence; but a loss of faith is not an inevitable consequence. Indeed, our loved one's death could compel us to look to our faith to make sense of this personal and incredibly painful loss. Instead of concluding that there is no God because, 'we cannot imagine that the God we thought we knew would do this to us,' we should remember that, having already recognised his helpfulness at other times, we can depend upon him in this, our greatest crisis thus far. We can draw strength also from the experience of the many people we know who have passed this way and, additionally, be encouraged by the strong testimony of God's people throughout the centuries. God is not going to withdraw his grace from us in these days of our greatest need.

Rarely does anyone enter into the bereavement experience with a realistic knowledge of what it entails. Those of us who have ministered to people through illness leading to bereavement might have believed we would cope more easily because of our experience but, in all probability, we will discover we have made a wrong assumption. Pastoral care teaches the pastor much, but the loss of wife or husband, child, relative or very close friend can be more traumatic than we ever imagined. The grief felt is often so traumatic that it cannot be marginalized; neither can its power to invade our hearts and minds be neutralised by an act of will. Nevertheless, our grief must be set in the context of a heavenly Father's love and concern for us and as part of his love and concern for all mankind. There are some very simple, basic thoughts that can help as we start adjusting to our new circumstances.

God has set a framework for our lives

Birth with its joys, life with its challenges and fulfilment and, finally, death with bereavement are all part of God's plan. The cycle of life and death established by God himself at the beginning of human life continues to run and will do so until the end of time. Our generation replaced that of our parents and in due course our generation will be replaced. Children outnumber centenarians because God planned endings as well as beginnings. The strategy is self-evident.

God's blueprint for our lives includes our place within a family structure. The family offers nurture, protection and the opportunity to live to our potential. Within the family the child discovers its identity as a person, learns how to relate to others, absorbs the family culture and faith, learns from example to become a responsible adult and, in turn, establishes his or her own family.

In his wisdom God planned that as we move in and out of the family home, we become part of a community. Made secure by our family base we find our livelihood within a wider group, find there our life's partner and work for the common good in a variety of ways, possibly even in the ongoing, encouraging life of the church.

It is important to add that this simple framework of life and death, family and community, does not stand unsupported. God himself surrounds and energises it by his power and presence. He delights in working out his eternal purposes in our human situation.

As Paul wrote: 'He (God) had his eye on us, had designs on us for glorious living, part of the overall purpose he is working out in everything and everyone' (Ephesians 1:11, *The Message*).

Within this framework there are no promises that our days will run smoothly. Even the length of our lives is uncertain. Life expectancy rates often provide encouraging reading but we have no reason to believe we will live as long as the national average indicates. By definition, the life expectancy age is not the minimum age. Bereavement is not restricted to the elderly. But, assuming we accept God's role in creating the framework for our lives: birth with its joys; life with its challenges, joys and satisfactions; death leading to bereavement and pain, we might well be tempted to ask why bereavement should be so painful.

The inevitability of pain

As well we know, every nerve end is sensitised by bereavement, every hope is crushed, in fact everything we cherish in life seems threatened. Bereavement hurts. But, having asked why it should be so painful, the best answer is most likely to be found in our capacity to love and love's power to bind people together.

The bonds of love with a child are there from the beginning, strengthened, at least for the mother by the self-giving, life-giving growth within the womb. As for the father, in his love, and with the evidence of the miracle of life taking place, he, too, is caught up in this mysterious process of bonding with his child.

Marriage is part of God's providential ordering for most people, if not all. When a man and woman are drawn to each other, and feel they are meant for each other, a relationship develops that is strengthened by a wide range of experiences leading to the mature commitment of marriage. Setting up a home, establishing a family, learning to build life together, caring for each other and the children through illness, as well as the joys and disappointments that are part of family life, help to make the bonds of love ever stronger.

When we love well, and have loved well through all the stages of life, and then husband, wife, child or sibling dies, it is a calamitous event. Inescapably, the experience is more than sorrow, it is heartbreak. It is more than pain, it is anguish. The reason for this incredible distress is simple and certain: great love + great loss = great pain.

To be without pain at bereavement could mean, possibly, that love has not been at the heart of the relationship: for to be without love in a relationship runs counter to everything God has planned. One of God's prime policies for the entire human race is that we should form relationships with each other. How poor are those people who have neither family nor friends! How rich we are when we have a stable family and a wide range of friends! But, in this complex realm of interactions, God planned

16

marriage and family relationships that transcend all other.

Although such relationships are common human experiences they feel quite original, and are remarkable for their ability to fulfil us to the depths of our being. It was God's intention that these bonds should be built on love, a love that continues to grow and satisfy as the years pass by. However marvellous at the beginning, a good marriage just keeps on getting better and, generally, this reflects itself in the quality of family relationships.

God has not specifically willed the pain in bereavement – but this all-pervading grief is inevitable once a loving relationship has been broken. In one sense, we would not have it otherwise. If bereavement's pain is the price of many – for some perhaps, not even many – rich and wonderful years of love, the pain is a price worth paying. Would we choose to be without those rewarding years to be without the present pain? The question evokes the emphatic answer – of course not! God planned the love – the pain is the natural consequence of our separation.

No heart more tender than a heart bereaved.
Shorn of its joy – its love-fulfilling dreams,
Facing new facts so hard to be believed,
With sadness, lost-ness, all consuming themes.

No heart more tender than one touched by
prayer,
Upheld by family love and praying friends –
By tenderness surrounded – Christly care –
A ministry of love that never ends.

No heart more tender than one firmly held
In Christ's two sorrow-scarred, yet powerful
hands,
Those hands with healing power unparalleled
Whose tender heart all heartache understands.

Our tenderness of heart – a gift from God
Who, in his Son, our paths of sorrow trod.

Heart to heart

In the months following my wife's passing most
of my poems related to that sad event. Within the
grouping there is a cluster of poems, including

some notes from my notebook that are particularly personal, but it seems appropriate to include them in this section.

We who are bereaved have become members of a wide-ranging community: our grief distinguishes us and binds us together. When heart speaks to heart all normal barriers disappear. We hear, not just the words but all the overtones of a shared experience. Were that all, it would be helpful, but it is more because the words strike responsive chords in our hearts imparting energy to our flagging spirits. As we share each other's sorrows, disappointments and hopes we realise that we speak each other's language. We are of value to each other.

'No one,' said Dean Eric Milner-White, 'can reach the heart of others except he speak from his own.' 'Heart to heart', therefore, is a fitting title for this selection of verses.

VULNERABLE

It comes, a spasm, hurtful, harrowing, Lord,
Involving body, mind and heart and throat,
   My frail defences overflowing, Lord,
And leaves me feeling ravaged and remote.

   It's not, Lord, that I look back with regret
At words not spoken or of deeds not done –
   Or words and deeds I try hard to forget –
Some argument I never should have won.

Our marriage, as you know was Heaven-made.
   We saw each other as your gift to us:
Strong was our love that time could never fade,
   A yielding love, concerned and generous.

   Our mutual support and tender touch,
Explain why I miss Win so very much.

WERE I TO DOUBT

Were I to doubt you, Lord, lack confidence
In who you are and in whose powerful hand
I find my comfort and my competence,
I would be lost, and mired in sinking sand.

In these, my hours and days of greatest need,
And mourning for the loss of my dear Win,
You have been with me step by step to lead
Me, where new heights of trustfulness begin.

You help me treasure all my memories;
You add fresh value to my priceless years,
And now, you add to my priorities –
I am to prove how well you answer prayers.

I am to draw much closer to your side
And live within the grace you will provide.

HOLDING FIRM

I need to walk with you, Lord, side by side,
I need to see what you see on life's way.
I need to be assured you will provide
All I require for this and every day.

Though I look back, O Lord, with gratitude
On life with Win, and all its rich rewards,
The forward-look must be my attitude,
And I must use the grace your plan affords.

It is your will that I mature should be,
More strong, more holy and more wise and true.
Win's death became my personal tragedy –
But you, Lord, take a different kind of view.

All you have planned for Win is now fulfilled,
While I press on to be the man you willed.

LIFE'S BREVITY

Today, we strew Win's ashes round a rose:
It is the customary thing to do,
A gesture helping families to close
The funeral rites and give all honour due.

Her ashes indicate life's brevity
And turn our eyes to God's great purposes;
To life's true value and eternity;
And help us understand who Jesus is.

For he, to us, proves death is not the end;
He proves that life has meaning and a goal
Beyond our human powers to comprehend.
Win's ashes stay, but onward goes her soul.

God works his miracles through human clay
And frees the soul for his eternal day.

THE ASHES

The ashes strewing-time was easier
Than my poor, tender heart thought it might be.
The moment called for something worthier
Than laying ashes round a chosen tree.

And yet, those moments eloquently spoke
Of Win's abiding love and influence,
And how, from death's brief pain-free sleep, she
woke
To see the glory of Christ's countenance.

Those ashes also told their story well:
Our earthly life is meant but to prepare
For life eternal, and the right to dwell
With Christ: his Heaven to know, his joys to
share.

The well-pruned 'Garden of Remembrance' rose
Blooms as a symbol of a love that grows.

THE PLAQUE IN THE CREMATORIUM
ROSE GARDEN

Winifred Read
1923 – 2007

Who loved so much –
and who was so much loved

THE MEMORIAL PLAQUE

Close to that yellow rose a plaque could stand,
Its message, by decree, must be quite brief.
A wordy tribute therefore, would be banned;
No space to write of faith, or hope, or grief.

Within that stricture, what then could we say
To indicate the essence of Win's heart,
A heart so finely tuned to God's own way,
A love, of God's own love, so much a part?

Then God, who loved Win, chose to be involved;
He gave the insight, rhythm and the word,
And with our problem heavenly resolved
The plaque declares the truth our hearts had
heard

And says of Win, in words which our hearts
moved:
'Who loved so much –
and who was so much loved.'

Lianne, one of our grand daughters, was expecting a child and she and her husband Paul had chosen the day for the public dedication of this new addition to our family. As is the way these days, they knew that a daughter, to be named Elise, was to be born to them. They asked me to write a song that could be sung by the congregation, which I did most gladly. The song was submitted to Lianne and Paul who expressed themselves pleased with it and Lianne got on with the business of being an expectant Mum.

Because Elise's birth was so eagerly and lovingly awaited, it seemed right and proper that the song should reflect those qualities and the first verse commenced:

It was a heavenly kind of day –
A day of glorious dawn.

I had forgotten the words of the song and only realised what I had written when, in the Dedication Service, we sang them. Was that really a 'heavenly kind of day – a day of glorious dawn'? Elise was born on 5th June 2007 and Win had collapsed and died in the early hours of that very day. Was it not rather, my darkest day?

When daylight dawned I had returned from the hospital and wrote the following email letter to inform my friends of the sadness that enveloped me.

5th June 07

Dear Friends,

This is a most difficult letter to write but I must make a start. It is now 5a.m. and I have just returned from the hospital.

Just after midnight Win collapsed and I called the Paramedics who came without delay and took her to the Bournemouth Hospital. In spite of the exceptional care Win was given she never regained consciousness. Whilst in the hospital Win had a cardiac arrest from which they resuscitated her but she faded quickly from that point and went to be with the Lord at about 3.30. Her passing was painless and we can be so glad about that. The medical staff were so very helpful and tender. They kept me informed of the treatment being given and I was able to spend time with her even though she was unconscious. What precious, albeit grieving, moments they were! How I will miss her!

It is not widely known that over the last couple of years Win had been receiving treatment for Alzheimer's disease. With her very positive spirit she had refused to surrender to this affliction even though its effects were becoming increasingly clear to see. Her diligence with crosswords, sudoku, code words and anything that would keep her brain active had to be seen to be believed. Win was a remarkable woman.

Win was incredibly sensitive to the needs of others, being of a most compassionate nature; she also had a great gift of prayer, spending a number of hours each day in intercession for the ever-growing number of names on her prayer lists.

I wrote a poem about this darkest day:

MY DARKEST DAY

The darkest, saddest day of all my days
Was when my darling Win collapsed and died.
I was confused – like standing in a maze –
My bearings gone – in need of God to guide.

And guide he did! His word to me was kept.
He gave me peace and gift on precious gift.
Though tears were shed as in my heart I wept,
On tides of grace God let my spirit drift.

Not once did God desert me in my need.
Though hurting from a wound both sharp and deep,
My wordless prayers began my cause to plead,
Unwaveringly he led – he did not sleep.

But with a constant flow of healing grace,
He made my wounded heart a trusting place.

THE DARKEST DAY OF MY LIFE?

How can God's mercy be described this way?
How can I thus define God's perfect will?
Win's work was done and ended was her day
And God had plans he wanted to fulfil.

Because of Alzheimer's Win's road was dark,
There was no further work for her to do.
Frail was her mind and frail her earthly barque
So God the anchor slipped and called her
through.

My sadness is eclipsed by Heaven's joy;
My pain transcended knowing she is healed;
My goal to faithful be in God's employ
And live my life as one whom God has sealed.

Win was called home. Dare I resent that call?
This day is not my darkest, after all.

BEST FOR ME ALSO

Dear Lord, I know your heavenly call to Win
Was right – your timing was impeccable,
You chose the time when Heaven should begin
And life from death would be the miracle.

Why then, O Lord, did I not realise
That what was best for Win is best for me?
Not for a moment did you move your eyes
From me; leave me from consolation free.

You love me, Father, and I am your child;
Your hand of mercy holds me in your care;
My needs and sorrows can be reconciled
Because both Win and I the same Christ share.

Lord, hold me even firmer in your hand.
O let me be the man your love has planned.

Summing up: It was a wonderful day for Win and, since I am also the focal point of God's love, it could not be my darkest day.

ABUNDANT GRACE

Your word reminds me, Lord, your grace is more
Than all my varied needs can ever be.
Your lightest touch of mercy can restore
A broken heart and give tranquillity.

If only this most finite mind of mine
Would grasp the truth that you are Sovereign
Lord;
That common clay by grace can be divine,
A treasure made of clay once badly flawed.

If only I could trust enough to reach
The goals for me, so generously set,
And let your gentle, Holy Spirit teach
Which truth to hold – what trivia to forget.

But, maybe, Lord, it is your well-planned choice
That I should choose each day to hear your
voice.

Another entry in my note-book says:

'This follows an attempt to define my grief but I found it painful and negative so I wrote, "Do not follow this through. Look rather to the positive will of God".'

I then restarted:

Bereavement is no accident – no punishment – no cross to bear. Bereavement is part of God's plan – his way of doing things.

I am not a lesser person because Win has gone

> Tender – yes;
>
> Bereft – yes;
>
> Missing her immensely – yes;
>
> In turmoil – no;
>
> Resentful – no;
>
> Self-pitying – no;
>
> Thinking gratefully – yes;
>
> Acting gratefully – yes.

Unless there is a remarkable happening one spouse dies before the other, one has to be left.

Did I think I would go first as men usually do? Yes.

Am I glad it was Win to go first? Yes.

Did I want her to go? No. I wanted to nurse

Win to the end or, at least until her memory loss was complete.

Did I want her to sink deeper into the depths of Alzheimer's? No.

Was God merciful? Yes.

Is he merciful? Yes.

What has he given you? A lifetime of joy with Win – everything in which to rejoice. All his promises to Win he has fulfilled; all his promises to me he is fulfilling.

What more can I ask for other than what he is doing for me? Nothing! He is the God of all-sufficient grace and that I have received, am receiving and will continue to receive until I, too am called home.

Be glad – rejoice – the Lord is good – His mercies endure forever.

I wrote further…

A TENDER GOD

God treats me tenderly,
Gently and lovingly,
Granting me all that I need.
Gives grace abundantly,
Wisely, effectively,
Even before I can plead.

He has great purposes,
Breathtaking strategies
In me he wants to instil,
Makes his firm promises
Based on realities
That I might follow his will.

He wants my heart to know
His life in me can grow
In spite of being bereaved.
Here on this earth below
Heaven's light in me can glow
As Jesu's life is received.

On November 9th I wrote in my notebook:

I seem to be more sensitive than ever to the absence of Win. Perhaps this is part of the natural order of experience regarding bereavement. I suppose I just need to cling on more – keep as close to the Lord as possible.

My life with Win, and Win's life with me was of God's ordering. Her death, and my life without her are still part of his providence – his constant care.

Since God is no man's debtor he will make up my loss in other ways. I must, therefore, look to those ways and be content.

Then I wrote:

IMMANENCE

The ever-present Father
Would have me be aware
That he is ever near me,
Surrounding me with care.
I never need feel lonely,
Distressed and valueless
Because in love he holds me,
My wounds to heal and bless.

Within his hallowing presence
Is all the grace I need,
Whatever be my challenge
In spirit, thought or deed.
He does not, cannot falter,
Since all that he can give
He places on the altar
For me to take, and live.

Because my God is present
In power, and care and love,
I must not be resistant,
But live his grace to prove.
The greater my dependence,
The firmer my hands hold.
The surer my obedience,
More mercies will unfold.

YOU OWE ME NOTHING, LORD

You owe me nothing, Lord. Have you not given
Me life, a vibrant Christian heritage,
Forgiveness for my sins, a glimpse of Heaven,
The gifts to live well on life's busy stage?

Did you not call me to a ministry,
A fruitful, self-denying way of life?
And, past my worth, my heart's expectancy,
Arranged that Win and I be man and wife?

When I consider what our marriage meant
To us, to family, to those we served,
The places we were destined to be sent,
The joyful, rich fulfilment, undeserved.

I can but say, you owe me nothing, Lord,
My life both was and is, one great reward.

A WORD FROM THE LORD

Lord, did you really say to me, 'Let Win go'?
Am I then holding tightly to the past?
Reluctant to allow my heart to know
That Win has moved on – is with you at last?

Are you, Lord, telling me that I too must
Accept your plans for Win are plans for me?
And, in those plans believe and fully trust
That Win's new life helps shape my destiny?

Of course I must be grateful for those years
That we were granted in our marriage bond,
Resist those thoughts that lead but to despair,
And concentrate on life – and life beyond.

I know O Lord, you want to make me whole
And keep my life firm in your strong control.

CHAPTER 1

LOVE IS MORE SIGNIFICANT THAN PERHAPS WE THINK

The true glory of human love is that it joins us with God who is the source of love. We can love purely, joyfully, sacrificially, unconditionally, and as near perfectly as flawed human beings can manage, only because God chose to make us in his own image.

God wants love, not power, not the wonder of creation, not even his majesty and authority to be seen as the quality that defines him. It was out of this love that God, the Father, sent his Son into our love-starved world. Through the life of Jesus, as well as in the pages of Scripture, the sheer splendour of God's love shines out; his love for the world (John 3:16), his love for his Son (Matthew 3:13-17), his love for those who love his Son (John 14:23), and the love we must show to each other (John 15:9-13). Because love is the dominant, motivating force within the heart of God, he has placed the capacity, and need, for love in our hearts. It is God's great aim that our love should mirror his love.

Our hearts, at their best, mirror God's intentions

Our present situation illustrates this powerfully. As we stood lovingly, helplessly and confusedly looking at those precious features from which life had departed, was there not an almost instinctive awareness that this is not the end? Had we been able to articulate our feelings would we not have said that the love that beat so positively within that now stilled heart must live on? Would we not have affirmed also that those capacities for goodness and joy could not be lost forever?

For many of us, held firmly within the trauma of those moments, it was not only an awareness of the finality of death that grew in our hearts. There was the hope, almost a conviction, that the personality that never failed to captivate us, and the dear one we loved totally and devotedly, must continue somehow, somewhere — and do so in a way that is rooted in, and yet transcends, our earthly life and ways.

However imperfect our understanding of love,
life's meaning, and God:

We have warm hopes of life beyond the grave;
    Our instincts point us to eternity.
Why else our souls disturbèd be and crave
    For knowledge of that vague reality?

We thirst, and water meets that simple need,
    We hunger, and we find food satisfies:
Our heart-felt thirst and hunger help us plead
For life beyond this life that Heaven supplies.

Creation has a nobler aim than death,
    And human personality demands
A worthier end to God's creative breath
    Than blinded humanism understands.

Death, therefore, matches not creation's goals:
So speaks God's living voice within our souls.

As our hearts take in the significance of what has
happened, and is happening still to us, life's trivia
fades and, in the forefront of our minds, the larger

issues of life and death emerge. Perhaps more than ever before, we feel that life has meaning and, intuitively, we move towards the possibility that life has been given its true meaning by the fact of death. If, as our hearts are telling us, death is not the end but a beginning, then both life and death have a potential far greater than anything we have imagined hitherto.

The more we see of death, the more we know
That death is a beginning, not an end;
The final barrier through which we go
Our destiny to find and comprehend.

Life has no meaning if love dies with death,
If, like our flesh, its qualities can waste;
Our hearts remind us: love breathes Heaven's
breath
Since God with timelessness our love has graced.

For death is but the soul returning home;
The well-worn key that opens up the door
Where love beyond imagining is known:
For Heaven is home – now and for evermore.

Death only seems to have the victory,
But God and Heaven are life's reality.

The heart then, is at its best when it confirms that love does not die: when it makes us value love — love in its highest form, the love that makes hope and even faith reasonable, desirable and, therefore, attainable. An awareness of these enduring qualities should help change the nature of our bereavement because we realise, more perhaps than ever before, that the human spirit rightly belongs to an order over and above our humanity, our tenuous hold on our mortality. It is an order that relates us to immortality, to God himself: the God whose love for us is such that he wants his kind of love to dominate us.

Once we allow that love does not die, an amazing new world begins to open its mysteries to us. It might appear extravagant to add that this discovery reveals the secret of the universe, but it would be true. With this insight we have been given the key to the meaning of life. We have begun to understand the heart and mind of God and because of that so much more lies ahead of us than behind us. Some people may smile indulgently at us but:

We are not fools for listening to our hearts

Of course our hearts tell us, and keep on telling us, we are hurting. They may tell us also that life is unfair and inform us that there isn't much sense in the timing of this tragedy. They may remind us too, that just when the full potential of our loved one's life was beginning to be fulfilled, it was drastically cut short.

These and related reactions are totally understandable. Not many people who are bereaved are going to create a persuasive rationale to justify the passing of their loved one! Love doesn't work that way and the aphorism remains true: great love – great loss – great pain.

But if the heart recognises the supremacy of love above all things, then it points us towards another world where human love will find its true meaning and expression in a realm where God reigns.

Therefore we must listen to our hearts.

The grief-producing love is also a heart-renewing love. Grief has the ability to disable us and disablement is not God's intention. This does not mean that a line can be drawn underneath our bereavement or that at some point in time we can conclude it is time to 'move on.'

Time will enable us to handle our grief more effectively although in one form or another we will continue to grieve.

But love is a positive, creative emotion. If there is a way of reconciling the past with the future, love will find it. Then, when in our sorrow we begin to see the tender shoots of hope, love will cherish and nourish them. God has not left himself without a voice in the human heart. He speaks through a variety of occurrences, but never more powerfully than when we realise that our love for our loved one relates us to him.

O MY SOUL!

Remember all that you are meant to be.
    You are not meant for mediocrity
    For life abundant is your destiny.

Within your secret depths did God not place
    A hope, conviction, whereupon to base
    A growing life of love, of faith and grace?

God gave to all your longings powers of speech,
    To all your insights, powers your heart to teach
    That he, Almighty God, is in your reach.

Become my soul, all that your God has planned,
    Live well and, trustingly at his command,
    Walk boldly, humbly holding firm his hand.

Our most worthy hopes and longings are consistent with his will for us. Most of us know that we tend to function at a level lower than our best yet there are times when we want to live on the higher level. For example: we recognise the transparent goodness of those who would be embarrassed if we described them as saints but who are, in actual fact, exactly that. In the nicest way we envy them and would like to have their strengths, gifts and influence, but feel that we are reaching above ourselves.

Of course we are reaching above ourselves! That's what God wants us to do. Our best longings are meant to encourage, not discourage us, because they are God-given and he longs to fulfil them.

The world's noblest souls listened to their hearts. Their godliest thoughts, liberated aspirations, and positive compassions set them, un-self-consciously, on the path of saintliness. We are free to become what God wants us to be, and what, in our heart of hearts, we would rather be.

Were we to listen to our hearts more, instead of to the cool words of those who think we are on this earth because of a myriad of chance-happenings in the universe, and not because we are part of some overriding plan of the Creator, we would live even better lives and in an even better world.

Faith hope and love are alive and well in the human heart. It is significant that St Paul remarked that these are the three characteristics that will ever abide and that the greatest of these is love (1 Corinthians 13:1 – 13). And we who try to read the message of the heart would agree.

God is in our hearts and in our thoughts

Although the poems in this section are largely sequential they do not reveal a steady move from despair to hope. Grief seems not to work that way: emotions are rarely logical. As though chosen at random, the elements of grief move repeatedly through our hearts and minds, focusing variously on our anguish, doubts and faith. Sometimes we are looking to God with a measure of hope and confidence; at other times we are not.

It is in the nature of grief to destabilise but, even so, our faith, aspirations and confidence in the love of God are never far away. Those stabilising factors can never be far away because God is with us, in our grief, hopes and faith.

BEREAVED BUT NOT BEREFT

I am bereaved, but I am not bereft.
The grieving consequence of death I feel
But God is loving and his hands are deft;
And tender is his touch my heart to heal.

My heavenly Father writes his love in me;
Unswervingly he claims me as his own.
His arms enfold me unconditionally
To grant the peace that comes from him alone.

My soul-mate I have lost just for a time –
The day of our reunion soon will dawn
But, I am not bereft! God's love is mine
Providing proof that death's sting is withdrawn.

God's promises forever he will keep;
Their benefits forever I will reap.

REALISM

I must not drift on turgid tides of sadness,
    My sullen sails bedraggled by despair.
No! I must ride the waves with hope and
           gladness
My swollen sails charged with celestial air.

My loved one lives! She has but gone before me.
    Her body's frailties are left behind,
She shares the life of Christ in highest glory,
    The fullness of her destiny to find.

What then of me? Do I my faith surrender?
Become a captive bound by memory's chains?
Can I not live enriched by memory's splendour
And prove in life and death that Jesus reigns?

Lift up this sometimes downcast heart of mine
O Lord, and in me let your glory shine.

OUR MORTALITY

Our frailty and mortality we see
As friends and loved ones walk death's lonely
vale.
Though we affirm our immortality,
Grief emanates from that much-trodden trail.

We know that life must end, e'er life commence,
That as the curtain falls upon this stage
Another rises on a scene immense;
A due reward for faithful pilgrimage.

We who are left, look to our memories;
Look up to God; reach out a trusting hand;
Look to our friends and to our families,
And find there's grace enough for us to stand.

In God's good time for us will come the morn,
When we will see the day eternal dawn.

WHEN CRIES MY HEART (1)

When cries the heart the blood seems turned to
tears
And pain made more intense as anguish swells:
The pain of loss – the pain of marvellous years –
The silent sounds, as loss its mystery tells.

When cries my heart its pain each sense
o'erwhelms;
Each gift is captive held in sorrow's thrall;
Each faculty an alien hand on helm.
All that I am obeys my heartache's call.

When cries my heart all else is meaningless;
What matters night or day or rain or sun?
My best achievements deemed as nothingness;
Made empty, any plaudits I have won.

When cries my heart I feel of little worth,
Distraught and frail, the loneliest man on earth.

WHEN CRIES MY HEART (2)

When cries my heart – I do not cry alone,
The wounds I bear are shared by Heaven's host;
My tears are seen and valued round God's
throne,
And God's true Father-heart feels it the most.

For our most tender God my anguish shares;
Not for my God, dispassion's care-less role.
Because he is my Father-God, he cares
And seeks to make my wounded spirit whole.

He touches tenderly and healingly
The deepest wound – the woes that in me rage.
I turn to him in need appealingly
And he gives grace my anguish to assuage.

He is the God of comfort and of peace
At whose strong word my fractious feelings
cease.

WHEN CRIES MY HEART (3)

When cries my heart, God hears and understands;
   My pain and loss he would expect to see.
   I am no puppet heeding his commands
   But flesh and blood and frail humanity.

   The Lord my God has promises to keep!
   He wants me faithful, fruitful to the end;
Determined, though the hills ahead be steep;
   Aware that he is with me: Friend with friend.

   He sees my sorrow as an open door
To vistas new and power beyond my thought;
To hands outstretched to take from him much
      more
Of grace, that I may know what he has wrought.

Death does not limit God – his love restrain,
   For in his hands death is eternal gain.

CHOSEN

I am the one you chose to be bereft,
To bear the weight of grief and loneliness,
So painfully aware that I am left
With memories and hopes that coalesce *(combine)*

Mine is the search for comfort and for peace,
The hope that puts a rainbow in the tear,
The faith and trust that ever seek release
From chains forged in the fires of doubt and fear.

Mine is the charge to prove love conquers death;
My life the lens that focuses the eyes
Of those who feel death's uninvited breath,
That they may see past death to Heaven's prize.

My strength must be the strength of faith
fulfilled,
The strength of one who lives as God has willed.

HELP FOR TODAY

O Lord, what are your plans for me today?
What graces will you bring from out my pain?
What insights give to help me on life's way?
What dross remove? What treasures to retain?

How will you turn my sorrow into joy?
My troubled thoughts and aspirations heal?
Will you this new experience employ
And with new acts of love my spirit seal?

How will you use this opportunity –
This vacuum in my life because of loss,
Ensuring all my days should fruitful be
And in me show the purpose of Christ's Cross?

Direct my soul and focus well my gaze
For I would serve you well all of my days.

JUST WHAT YOU WILL, LORD

Just what you will, Lord. That is best for me.
My lack of wisdom means I cannot make
The right decisions for my destiny.
In you, Lord, I must trust and your ways take.

And, if at times I question what you say,
Behave as though your will for me is flawed,
Then, do forgive me, Lord. Point out the way
Whereby, through simple faith I name you Lord.

I think, Lord, tension comes because my heart
Accepts your rule, but feels the pain of loss.
Unbidden, tears of tenderness just start –
Perhaps, just like your tears at Jesu's Cross?

If my sad heart displays its deep distress,
It does not mean, O Lord, I trust you less.

GOD'S WORK WITH ME

Again, I ask the crucial question, Lord,
What changes do you want to see in me
If I accept, as written in your word,
That you are pruning me more fruit to see?

It is your way to use each circumstance
Of good or ill, whatever I may meet,
My gifts, my dedication, to enhance
So that in me your plans may be complete.

With this sharp pruning, Lord, what must I shed?
What new-found skill to justify this pain?
Down which new avenue will I be led
To turn my grievous loss to heavenly gain?

For new adventures, Lord, my soul prepare
And new achievements in both deed and prayer.

SUSCEPTIBILITY

I think, Lord, I'm susceptible
To feeling sorry for myself.
My heart seems indefensible
'Gainst anxious thoughts that come by stealth.

My weaker, human side persuades
Me to adopt the victim's role,
But in your light that concept fades,
Since you, O Lord, must rule my soul.

For victim-hood is foolishness,
And through your offered, boundless grace
You seek each new-born day to bless,
And make my heart a bonding place.

Then, with my new unclouded eyes
Let me perceive your grand design,
And through my sorrow recognise
That pain, in your hands, is divine.

CAUGHT UNAWARES

It would be wrong, unusual in fact
If, now bereaved, emotions were not stirred.
This can be done by someone's lack of tact,
A hug, a look, a sympathetic word

And, suddenly, my feelings run amok,
My eyes and throat and voice are uncontrolled.
My mind advises me: calm down, take stock,
Bring all those feelings back into the fold,

Let measured thought and common sense
prevail,
You are the centre of God's love and grace.
Be not afraid of tenderness, or fail
To know God holds you firm in his embrace.

Whatever may be said, implied or done
Whate'er your struggle be – the fight is won.

A LEARNING PROCESS

I'm slowly learning, Lord, that human grief
Submits not to a human discipline.
In spite of deep, long-verified belief,
The war with feelings is so hard to win.

Beneath the smile, the statement, 'I can cope'
Lie swirling tides of sadness and of pain,
In part controlled by discipline and hope,
But waiting chance to prove their strength again.

Perhaps this is the price one has to pay
For all the joy a perfect marriage brings?
If so, the price is worth it, come what may
For to the saddest heart, such joy gives wings.

Why should not grief be deemed as positive?
It is by love and pain and joy we live.

ANOTHER DAY

Another day of sorrow and of pain!
Another day o'ershadowed by my loss,
Another day as loss is turned to gain
As hope I draw from Jesus' hope-full cross.

We learn so much from heartache and from
stress.
Learn much about ourselves and more of God.
We are made strong when hardships 'gainst us
press
Which strengthen us to bear our grievous load.

These then are days for trusting in the Lord,
Receiving grace and God's own joy and peace,
Of being valued, loved and owned – though
flawed,
Of knowing God's great mercies will increase.

Another day of opportunity:
Of life and hope, of faith and victory!

A DIFFERENT SCALE OF VALUES

Our times of grief are precious to our God.
They show our tenderness – our inmost love.
Though grief and pain walk with us on our road
Those qualities our hidden strengths can prove.

Not ever would we think grief's path is smooth –
How could it be when we have lost so much?
But God has grace, each trembling heart to
soothe
And healing flows from his compassionate
touch.

How can he make us strong if we feel not
The pressures of our weakness deep within?
Since we are human, is it not our lot
To feel the hurts that help new life begin?

O how I need you, Lord, to set my feet
On that blest road where pain and joy can meet!

I OWE YOU EVERYTHING, O LORD

I owe you everything, O Lord, my God.
All that I am and have, I owe to you:
Life's straightening path, the roads yet to be trod,
The passing years and Heaven's most glorious
view.

Whatever good there is within my soul,
Whatever light may shine behind my eyes,
Those vibrant signs that life is now made whole
Have been, and are, due to your enterprise.

Age has not wholly quenched the flames of
youth;
These later years your quickening fires have felt.
You gave the strong desire to know your truth
And through the years in your love I have dwelt.

It is a fact, Lord, everything I owe
To you: my power to be, to do, to know.

CHAPTER 2

HOW, THEN, DO WE BEGIN TO COPE WITH BEREAVEMENT?

Inevitably, the early days are marked by turmoil and we struggle because our feelings and perceptions are clouded by pain and sadness. Conversations with the funeral director, minister, family and friends have an air of unreality about them because the fact of bereavement is hard to assimilate.

But bereavement is the reality, and we know we are going to have to live with it and the prospect of doing so is a massive burden. Questions related to coping with this unwelcome situation add their weight to the burden, but another truth waiting to be discovered is that the burden only *seems* to be beyond our capacity.

In fact we have enormous reserves of endurance and hope: all so generously given by God. For a time negative feelings may continue to dominate us, and the positive feelings of hope and confidence appear to have perished, but hope and confidence will rise again.

Our heavenly Father has not abandoned us to our distress. He knows our struggles and stands beside us in them, remaining true to his purposes. Furthermore, and crucially, God does not see bereavement as a life sentence to a state of sorrow and despair. Rather, he sees it as a process, an important part of our journey of life. It is a journey our wise and loving God wants us to commence but he knows that our starting time should not be hurried.

We should try to remember God is still with us
Taking each day as it comes is an essential part of the process. Every journey commences with the first step, then one step at a time and one day at a time, keeps us in line with God's will for us. Our days of sorrow and near despair may not be over for quite some time but, though we are struggling, we are not left to struggle alone. One day, perhaps, we may even see that our journey in bereavement has so many positive spiritual overtones that it has become a pilgrimage.

Quite remarkably, this Almighty God who is our Heavenly Father walks each step of this difficult path of bereavement with us. The words of the psalmist, possibly read at your loved one's funeral, are relevant, not only in a funeral service, but now.

'Even though I walk through the valley of the shadow of death, I will fear no evil, for you are with me' (Psalm 23:4).

Observe that in the valley it is the shadow – *the shadow only* – of death that oppresses us. Shadows only exist where there is light and the light above the valley is God's light, and soon, sooner probably than later, that light will shine. Francis Thompson in his great poem, *The Hound of Heaven*, in which he details his spiritual aspirations and frustrations asks the highly perceptive question, 'Is my gloom after all, shade of his hand outstretched caressingly?' Thompson was in the process of learning that God is with us in the darkened valley experience, and that his love is constant.

There are other words of Jesus, possibly read also at your loved one's funeral, that are most helpful and hugely important.

'Do not let not your hearts be troubled. Trust in God; trust also in me. In my Father's house are many rooms; if were not so, I would have told you.

I am going there to prepare a place for you. And if I go and prepare a place for you, I will come back and take you to be with me that you also may be where I am' (John 14:1-3).

Clearly, in bereavement, our hearts are troubled: they can hardly be otherwise. On any scale of stress, anywhere in the world, the loss of a loved one generates the greatest and most sustained tension. Any words, therefore, that help us to handle this stress are exceedingly valuable.

The word that is translated 'troubled' means to stir or to agitate. Our Lord is saying, in effect, that we have a measure of control over our feelings. Not total control obviously: it doesn't take a great deal to re-energise our grief.

Our sorrow can be triggered by a simple act even as we reorganise our home. The sorrow can return when a salesperson phones and asks for our loved one by name; or a letter will come; or a friend, unaware of our loss, will ask concerning his/her well-being.

The occasions are varied and numerous, but Jesus tells us not to *stir up* our feelings of grief. We need to learn how to avoid venturing into those highly sensitive areas that would leave us weaker rather than stronger.

Sometimes we feel like talking about our bereavement. Sometimes we don't and, if we don't feel like talking, we don't have to. Our friends, in their thoughtfulness usually sense that and co-operate well: they know when to withdraw gracefully. Within the family circle there are few limitations but, outside of the family and/or a special friendship, it might be a long time before we feel able to talk freely about ourselves.

Jesus is not suggesting that we do not mourn or that we stifle grief, or deny the pain. Wisely, he is saying, do not exacerbate the situation; do not agitate the various elements of your sorrow; do not make your feelings unbearable. Occasions to grieve come often enough but, because grief can be destructive, our Lord says simply that we should take care not to make things worse.

To stir emotions that should not be stirred
Is not the wisest thing for me to do.
If those strong feelings swirl round undeterred,
More anguish, tears and heartache will ensue.

Christ does not say I should not mourn or grieve,
Nor try denying my bereavement's pain.
I should not stir my grief he says – but leave
My pain un-churned to minimise the strain.

He knows so well what I am slow to learn
That he has grace for every day's demands
And if, in simple trust, to him I turn
I find he holds me safely in his hands.

My grief is real – but so is Jesus' grace –
And he speaks peace in my heart's secret place.

Jesus goes on to say, 'Trust in God; trust also in me.' In effect, he is asking us to look beyond our present troubles, massive though they are, to the greatest power, the highest authority, to God himself. If we cannot trust the Creator, the source of all goodness, the wise, compassionate, architect of providence, who can we trust? We lift, therefore, our troubled hearts and empty hands to God and affirm our trust in him then, trusting him, we trust also the Lord Christ who came to reveal the love of the Father to us. For Jesus assures us that, because he and the Father are the essence of love, we can trust them and, unlikely as it may feel to us, everything is going to be all right. Both in the temporal and eternal scheme it really is going to be all right.

Jesus continues: 'In my Father's house are many rooms; if it were not so, I would have told you. I am going there to prepare a place for you.'

The most gracious, believable and powerful person who has ever walked on earth confirms our hope that there is another life after death. Jesus goes into no detail but makes it clear that we will not lose our identity. He implies that who and what we are matter to such a degree that there will be a place just for us. No bland, mass-produced, never-ending celestial conurbation awaits us, but the location is with him and he determines the quality of our lives:

'And if I go and prepare a place for you, I will come back and take you to be with me that you also may be where I am.'

How very reassuring for us! The above statement is paraphrased by Kenneth Taylor in the *New Living Bible* as, 'When everything is ready I will come for you,' which is even more comforting. That is, more comforting for those of us whose lives have more or less run full term and we can accept the fact that we are being called and taken home.

At certain times, death comes to us as friend;
   With gentleness he stands inside the room;
      He tells that burdens now are at an end
   And, in the name of Jesus, whispers, 'Come',

Earth's open door is closed without a sound
   While life, as mortals know it, is no more,
   And opened is the door to Heaven's ground
Where reigns the King whom heavenly hosts
      adore,

Where all is peace and glory's purest light –
   The air, song-filled with joy and praise,
   Where trophies of God's grace and love and
      might
Pay tribute to God's kindness and God's ways.

But the foregoing statements take no cognisance of untimely deaths: those caused by war or criminal acts, or accidents, illness, congenital faults and the like. So many have had no cause to be ready to be called home but, even so, the un-timeliness of the deaths does not take Christ out of the situation.

Can his welcome be less real because of the shorter duration of life or unusual circumstances of the passing? Surely not! Christ calls those whose time has come: and those whose deaths are untimely, he receives. He who encourages us to trust in him will not fail us in the decisive hour.

God's grace matches our needs

There are some things God can only do for us when we are in difficult and demanding situations. The underlying principle is: the greater our need, the greater his demonstration of grace and power. We cannot heal our own brokenness of heart. That is clear. Neither can we, unaided, put this massive event in perspective. We can try the stoical, stiff-upper-lip routine that sometimes convinces others we are coping well but we ourselves remain unconvinced. We can, as some people have tried, part-close our minds to the future and live on our memories. In this regard, the beautiful, haunting words of Alfred, Lord Tennyson commend themselves and enthral us:

> 'But, O for the touch of a vanished hand,
>   And the sound of a voice that is still!'

How wonderfully well the couplet expresses our longings! If only… if only… we sigh, but Tennyson's inspired and superbly crafted lines echo the past and do little to help us into the days ahead. In spite of all our nostalgia we have to reach out to the future because, hopefully, we are beginning to see, or soon will see, that bereavement is more than a static condition and circumstance, it is part of an ongoing process.

God makes realistic promises of help

We have so many needs at this time: courage, peace, comfort, reassurance, healing of the heart, and the ability to cope with loneliness. In addition we have to handle the essential duties at a time when we are pressured enough. Perhaps also, our feelings of inadequacy cloud our awareness of a heavenly Father who has made promises to his people: promises that he wants us to claim at a time like this. God will not mind if we look to him to redeem his word. The truth is that he is always at hand and that he comes to us with his invaluable aid.

A promise of peace

Before he left The Upper Room to be arrested, tried and crucified, Jesus said to the disciples – and through them, to us, 'Peace I leave with you; my peace I give you. I do not give to you as the world gives. Do not let your hearts be troubled and do not be afraid' (John 14:27). It is possible to have his peace even though it feels as though our world has collapsed around us. Amazingly, in the midst of all the turmoil his peace stands firm. The peace of God then, is for all occasions including the hardest of times.

A promise of his presence

Our friends come to us in our need because they love us, feeling their inability to help us except by their presence – and how we need their presence – but our heavenly Father draws near with total ease because he has the grace to help us at this most difficult time. He, and only he, can meet our needs.

From the earliest days of God making himself known to his people, he has promised his presence: 'I am with you and will watch over you... I will not leave you' (Genesis 28:15). Throughout Scripture this promise is reinforced, 'When you pass through the waters, I will be with you; and when you pass through the rivers, they will not sweep over you. When you walk through the fire you will not be burned...' (Isaiah 43:2). Comfort is found also in the Psalms: 'The Lord is close to the brokenhearted and saves those who are crushed in spirit' (Psalm 34:18), 'The Lord is near to all who call on him' (Psalm 145:18).

The Scriptures make clear that God has feelings and because he is exposed to suffering he can identify with us as we suffer. The concept of the loving kindness, the tender compassion of God, is not new. The prophet Isaiah expressed this powerfully as he gave a word-picture of Jesus hundreds of years before Jesus came to earth, 'But he was pierced for our transgressions, he was crushed for our iniquities; the punishment that brought us peace was upon him, and by his wounds we are healed' (Isaiah 53:5). The compassions of God are vital to us since they offer shelter and resources and are a guarantee of our continual well-being.

I hide me in the feelings of my God
Who loves me with an everlasting love.
Who walks with me along my pilgrim road
And seeks in me his love and grace to prove.
All that I need awaits my earnest prayer,
All that I am is safe within his care.

As we depend more and more on our Heavenly Father, the process of bereavement becomes more reassuring and maturing. God shares our feelings and provides his all-sufficient grace. The key to all the help we need is found in God's grace: a grace that has been defined as the undeserved favour of God. We are certainly undeserving: but our heavenly Father is generous.

A promise of strength

It is one of the paradoxes of the Christian faith that when we are at our weakest we can be at our strongest. If, in our helplessness, we turn to God and trust in him, he gives us the strength we need to cope. It was out of a deep experience of personal weakness that Paul gave an insight from God that has stood the test of every generation since. 'But he (God) said to me, "My grace is sufficient for you, for my power is made perfect in weakness".'

Paul then lists some of his problems and concludes 'For when I am weak, then I am strong' (2 Corinthians 12:9, 10).

This simple, working principle can prove itself true in our current stress. Unaided we will fail but, empowered by the grace of God, we will move, slowly perhaps, falteringly, almost reluctantly, but move we will through this bewildering process. Frances Ridley Havergal wrote a hymn making each verse start with the same statement, 'I could not do without thee,' and makes one of her verses end with the couplet:

> And weakness will be power,
> If leaning hard on thee.

Sometimes we find praying is difficult

Bereavement can be so overwhelming and disorienting that many people, even some who have had a very active prayer-life feel that prayer, at this time, is beyond them. Our heavenly Father will have no problem with that. He is the one who reads the heart and knows our feelings better than we know them ourselves. Consequently, he provides for us by the prayers of his people. Not only those known to us are interceding on our behalf, making the prayers we feel unable to pray, but there are some people who have a special gift of prayer and who fulfil their gift through their ministry of prayer. Is it not true also that in times of great stress we often have an awareness that we rest, if that is the right word, on a cushion of prayer?

More than that however, and again we are indebted to Paul for the insight, 'In the same way, the Spirit (the Holy Spirit) helps us with our weakness. We do not know what we ought to pray for, but the Spirit himself intercedes for us with groans that words cannot express' (Romans 8:26).

But that is not all! Not only is the Spirit praying for us, but the Lord Christ is himself an intercessor. Before he left the Upper Room to go to Gethsemane and then to Calvary, in a great prayer of intercession Jesus prayed for those of us who, in time, would believe on him (John 17:20). In his letter to the Romans, Paul helps us by reminding us that, 'Christ Jesus … is at the right hand of God and is also interceding for us' (Romans 8:34). The writer to the Hebrews also reiterates this truth: 'therefore he (Jesus) is able to save completely those who come to God through him, because he always lives to intercede for them' (Hebrews 7:25). In our need and frailty, God makes provision for us.

God values us too much for us to fail

It is because of our worth to God that he planned us to be the pinnacle of his creation. The love that created those near and distant stars did not give them the capacity to love. The relationships between the heavenly bodies are probably crucial

84

to the balance of the universe, but those relationships are functional, not loving. Our value therefore, is not to be compared with whirling masses of rock or gas in outer space, because we live on a more significant level. We relate to God himself, the Creator, the heavenly Father who made us in his own image and decreed that our love should be like his love, and that all our relationships should have that same quality.

As human beings, we are the highest form of life God created. Our personalities are complex, our potential immense with our freedom to be evil and our freedom to be saintly. We are drawn towards self-indulgence – we are drawn towards God – to be indwelt by his love and to love like him. And our loving, heavenly Father draws near to us in our distress. As we allow him to do so, he gives us the grace we need to look backward with gratitude and forward with hope. It is why he wants our bereavement to be a process – a journey – and why he is with us all the way.

CHAPTER 3

UNTIMELY DEATHS

The death of a child: its mystery and sorrow

In the comparatively early days of our marriage my wife, Win, and I shared the loss of a son, our second child. In those days it was often possible for a child to be born in a maternity home where mother and child would stay for a few days. In such a helpful situation our son was born.

He was healthy, handsome – of course – and brought us much joy and satisfaction. Win and Peter – the name long chosen for him – were due to return home on a Saturday morning but, because the matron knew I would be taken up with the responsibilities of our congregation over the weekend, she suggested that I collect them on the Monday morning. It was a thoughtful gesture that had immense consequences.

Viruses have never been absent from hospitals and maternity homes and in those additional hours Win spent in the home, a virus infected our newly-born son. Because his immune system was undeveloped the infection proved fatal and we had to cope with the loss of this already much-loved child.

As with all other parents, our love had grown with his anticipated birth. It was a love that would never be fulfilled. Our faith remained firm but it was a hard experience and, although it happened many years ago our memories of and love for our newly-born and newly-lost child remain forever fresh in our hearts.

A DEEP GRIEF AND SADNESS

Some things, our hearts can hardly understand,
Stern facts that seldom can be reconciled;
We cannot think that these the Lord has
planned,
Especially, the passing of a child.

If God is love, how can this sadness come?
How can he let this tragedy take place?
Our hearts feel pain – our minds feel numb;
If only we could feel his healing grace!

But healing grace is closer than we know;
The Christ who bore our suffering on the cross
Has grace enough, our hearts to overflow
And love enough, to share with us our loss.

Although the mysteries of death remain,
Within the saddest heart Christ's peace can
reign.

DESPAIR

O God, I turn to you in my despair –
I do not even know if you exist
Or, if existing, you can know or care
Enough to know that I am so distressed.

No parents should be called on to endure
The pain of knowing that their child has died,
A pain for which there seems to be no cure,
A pain that hour by hour is magnified.

It seems illogical, O God, a waste
Of every precious value we have known.
This is the biggest trial we have faced
And, seemingly, must face it on our own.

If you be God, it is to you I turn,
Subdue the fires of grief that in me burn.

THE SUDDEN DEATH OF A CHILD

That peaceful child, eyes closed, is not asleep,
Unless for death, sleep is a synonym.
He is at peace, while our hearts vainly weep
And long that we could give new life to him.

It seems so pointless that a child should die,
That having come to healthy, natural birth,
He should without a cry, without a sigh
Surrender his potential here on earth.

We are surrounded by great mysteries,
We could lose faith, did we not know of Christ,
Who fought 'gainst pain and death as enemies,
And for our victory was sacrificed.

In Heaven, God will life's circle make complete,
And round his throne our family we will meet.

The death of one who has so much more to give

Now, as an octogenarian I mourn for my darling wife, Win, who passed from this life on 5th June 2007. A few days earlier we had celebrated our 57th Wedding Anniversary.

Our marriage was so good that, like many other people similarly blessed, we believed it had been made in Heaven. But, if as a family we imagined we would be spared the stress of further loss for some time, events were to prove otherwise.

Almost a year after Win's passing, and late in the evening of 9th May 2008, I received a phone call telling me that my son-in-law Graham, who had shown no sign of illness, had suddenly died. One moment he was part of a conversation with his wife and a couple of friends, the next moment he had gone and could not be revived.

Graham was a gifted, family-oriented man, much loved by his wife and family and not least by my wife and me. In consequence as a family we were plunged deeper into the experience of bereavement.

Tragic and painful though this is, it is not unusual. Life so often seems to be taking its normal course and then the unexpected happens. There is an unforeseen physical problem, an accident, an act of mindless violence or of war, a natural disaster and, at whatever age, bereavement becomes the unwelcome experience of a new widow or widower, or parents and family. Within the community the mourning process also commences as people who are bound together by ties of friendship or association feel and express their loss.

QUESTIONS

Some questions, Lord, keep forming in my mind
Regarding the un-timeliness of death.
How blind death is! Unutterably blind
To take my loved one full of life and health.

We had so much and had much more to give,
We had such prospects, so much joy ahead,
Life was so full and we knew how to live
But now, I see a future full of dread.

Why do some people use their liberty
To do those things that others maim and kill?
Why are they free to act so wilfully
And leave a vibrant life forever still?

A dangerous gift our gift of freedom is,
With power to end life's possibilities.

FUTILITY

It is the vacuum, Lord, the emptiness:
Our lives were full, complete, with more to
come,
But my belovèd died – then came the stress
And all that's left in life is wearisome.

It's not, Lord, that I'm angry or distraught,
I just can't see why this should have to be.
All that is best in life has come to naught,
My every thought fraught with uncertainty.

Do I blame you, O Lord, or blame mere chance?
Do all things bow to your supreme control
Or could some maverick circumstance
Elude your touch and sear with fire my soul?

I look for comfort. Do I look in vain?
If you are God, can you not ease my pain?

GRIEF

There is a grief which tears the soul apart,
When love has lost the object of its love.
And in that partial vacuum of the heart
The tensions and the pressures painful prove.

To lose one's love, by pain and dread disease –
Observe the wastage of that once strong frame,
Be left, in middle-life, with memories
Must all the heart's deep senses hurt and maim.

And yet — for there must ever be 'and yet' –
Though death and loss must mystery remain,
Our suffering Lord would have us not forget
That through such pain and loss, come hope and
gain.

He is the burden bearer for us all,
He holds us firm. He will not let us fall.

AN ATTEMPTED ANSWER

God does not will bereavement's bitter pain:
He is a God of grace, a God of love.
But in our world, so much that causes strain
And grief is made by us, as happenings prove.

So many things have consequences dire:
Deliberate evil cannot be God's will,
Events created by corrupt desire
Can hardly help our Lord his will fulfil.

But God is nigh and, though bad things occur,
To all who will receive, he offers grace.
Most generously on us he will confer
The comforts needed in our heart's most secret
place.

Our God is not remote but near at hand
To help us in each circumstance to stand.

EPILOGUE

In ordinary use an epilogue indicates closure. It is the end of a book, a play or a programme, a neat, acceptable way of ensuring that readers, audience or participants have a satisfying sense of completeness. However, in the Christian life there is never a final chapter or a concluding scene. On our stage the curtain comes down, only to be raised again for our lives to be truly consummated in eternal life. Clearly, our heavenly Father doesn't do epilogues – but he amazes us with his provision of new beginnings.

For our loved one then, this is not an epilogue but another prologue

The future God had planned has been realised. Life's last great battle has been won; the last great enemy has been overcome and, in John's powerful phrase, our loved one has 'passed from death to life' (1 John 3:14).

Whatever the manner of that passing: frail, hesitant, courageous, eagerly anticipated or sudden, it has been life's final, defining adventure.

Not for any other person the swooping down of the chariot of fire in the kind of whirlwind that took Elijah from earth to Heaven (2 Kings 2:11) but for everyone else so far, it has been something much more commonplace, even though the transition from earth to Heaven has been no less real.

And if, as we imagine, the trumpets sounded on the other side for Elijah, they sounded no less triumphantly for the one we loved.

Had we the ears – we would have heard the
trumpets sound,
And heard the Christ's, 'Well done!' upon that
distant ground.

At this early stage in our bereavement, however, our thoughts are sombre as befits an epilogue, rather than bright with the hope and optimism of a prologue – and that is perfectly understandable. It is not easy in the pain and confusion of these grieving days to step back a little and try to see the big picture of God's dealings with us but, if, and when, we can do so, the attempt is valuable.

On the first Christmas Day after my wife's passing, as I was meditating on the change bereavement had made to this previously joyful celebration, it occurred to me that it is possible to focus so intently on the detail of a heart-rending grief, that the large picture of God's strategy becomes distorted.

Bereavement all our concepts can distort
But, seen within God's plans for all mankind
We can discern his wise and loving thought
Through which our life's true destiny we find.

Christ came to earth God's vision to fulfil,
That we should share with him eternity;
Think his great thoughts; express his perfect will
As children in his heavenly family.

If we could see through God's all-loving eyes
More things on earth with Heaven would
harmonise.

Because the heavenly goal has been reached, marking a new beginning for our loved one, this confirms the thought that this is a prologue.

All the wonders, joys, glories of Heaven lie ahead.

There are no tears, neither is there pain, chronic illness, terminal disease, confusion or forgetfulness in Heaven. Instead, there is wholeness and the fulfilment of John's awe inspiring insight, 'we know that when he appears, we shall be like him, for we shall see him as he is' (1 John 3:2b).

The Bible says much about Heaven, but not enough for us to have a definitive picture. We know that it is the home of our Almighty God and the realm where Christ is King. We know also that he has prepared a place for us and that those who have chosen his way are to be with him forever. Furthermore, we believe that our loved one is sharing in all the wonderful adventures and glories that Heaven affords.

Our earthly pilgrimage leads to Heaven

Although the concept of Heaven challenges our comprehension it must be true that God intended our time on earth to be an adequate preparation for eternity. Of the many facets of life that help make us aware of our final destiny it may be that those mysteries some of us call miracles play a crucial part. From the beginning to the end of life there are miracles – many more perhaps than we realise, while Heaven must be utterly alive with them.

There is the miracle of human birth,
Another child delivered to our earth:
The miracle of personality
With love to fill the soul's capacity.

There is the miracle of human death
When God withholds the life-sustaining breath,
And breathes the breath of Heaven in the soul
To make that life, by heavenly standards, whole.

And then, the greatest miracle is done,
With darkest valley passed, and Heaven won,
God reaches out his hand in love to bless
And grants his faithful children, Christlikeness.

To look into the eyes of Jesus and receive his welcome; to bow before the Father; to see the sights of Heaven, hear its sounds, the glories of its language; to be part of its fellowship and worship must be astounding. Human words are inadequate for a prologue for such a life – but prologue this is nevertheless.

If this is a prologue for our loved one – it is a prologue for us also

It is only too true that when the unthinkable happened and our loved one died, we knew immediately that life could never be the same again. Our bruised and thwarted expectations may tell us that, from now on, everything we attempt and experience, can only be second best. At this time, despair, pain and loss tend to sum up the human level of perception and it seems irrational, insensitive, and inappropriate to the point of being inadmissible, even to imply that there is a way ahead.

Even so, the big picture shows that God is pursuing his dream for mankind. If, as our hearts would have us know, love does not die and death is not the end for our loved one, we would not be surprised to learn that our forward-looking God has plans for us throughout this sad and painful time. These plans represent the divine level of perception and, as this insight gradually dawns on us, we will begin to see why bereavement is a process, a journey, rather than a state.

Knowing that we need time to grieve, God allows us as much time as we need. He knows our capacities far better than we know them ourselves and his time-frame recognises the requirements, the rhythms and nuances of our lives: he knows the pace that suits us best and works accordingly. Mercifully, in our difficult and inescapable days such as a birthday, a wedding anniversary, Christmas Day and, not least, the anniversaries of the death and funeral, God shows his patience and gentleness. Those days are very tender and are made even more so because of our heavenly Father's tenderness.

As for the future, it will be different from the past but it is a future that will honour God; honour our loved one who has preceded us to Heaven, and honour us also. By God's design we are unique within creation possessing a spiritual potential far beyond our understanding. Consequently, if we allow, he will reinforce our intuitive aspirations, reawaken our faith, to enable us achieve more in the days ahead than we imagined possible.

God does not waste our bereavement experience

As time passes – oh so very slowly – we become aware that we are being built up again. We begin to realise that God is doing what he does so well, which is to take even our painful, unsought experiences and turn them into something very precious. Neither does he waste our tears or devalue our feelings of desolation. Instead, and most remarkably, he takes the various features of our mourning and – dare we say this – uses them for our benefit and to his glory?

GOD WASTES NOTHING *thing Spoiled in making*

God is no wastrel – each experience
We have, a treasured harvest-time can yield. *destructive*
And even things with baleful consequence
Can be transformed – and his love be revealed.

He does not waste bereavement's grief and
stress!
The tears that cloud the eye and gently fall
He uses to increase our tenderness –
Fits us to hear another's plaintive call.

The grief that racks the body and the soul
Is precious too. God uses it to draw
Us close to Christ – with him in grief enrol;
With him the depths of costly love explore.

As we, in weakness, on our God depend
Our lives begin God's mercies to commend.

God cannot waste our grief because he is the source, the essence, of love, and grief is part of love. Since all aspects of the nature of God are positive it follows that grief is not – or should not be – a negative experience but the means of fruitful, ongoing attainment.

Mysteriously and wonderfully, our tenderness, pain and grief link us upward to God and outward to so many people who suffer as we are suffering. When we are ready, we will find God waiting to use our most unwelcome experiences to help others. In our own bereavement many people expressed sympathy and it was greatly appreciated, but the sympathy that really counted was that which came from people who had themselves been bereaved. Because they know the sorrow, the almost crippling distress of bereavement, they spoke with understanding and authority and, because they are still walking this way, they became our role models, showing us that though much has been lost, much of value remains. It is part of our privilege, consciously or unconsciously, to show others how to handle grief.

God does not waste the life and influence of our loved one

The way ahead for us does not involve 'drawing a line under this experience' as if it was just another large disappointment we are to regard as a bad experience and 'move on'. Bereavement is not part of the baggage of life, rather it is part of the whole of life for us. By his gracious providence God has a way of binding the past, present and future together. Are we not better people because of the give-and-take nature of this special relationship with our loved one? Does not the enormity of our loss indicate how greatly we have been enriched by it? Are we not wiser, more discerning, more mature and rounded in our personalities? Has not our loved one helped to shape, for the better, what we have become and what we will become in the years ahead? Do we not live each day by the faith we shared, the lifestyle we jointly developed and owned? Do we not still see ourselves as an entity being true to our joint standards and aims in life? Nothing wasted there!

God does not waste a grief-generated compassion

On innumerable occasions we have been moved when tears and tenderness have been transmuted into compassion, and the pain of bereavement has become gain for those who suffer the same disease or disability as their loved one suffered. With courage, resourcefulness and great energy, hospices have been established and funded; holiday homes for children established; half-way houses for a variety of addicts set up; money for research in a wide range of disease, specialist equipment identified, paid for and dedicated in hospitals; while trusts have been established for this, that and the other need. The list is endless. Undoubtedly, as we allow him, God turns loss into gain; sorrow into joy; frustration into fulfilment. He wastes nothing; not our tears, love, frustrations, fears, memories, hopes, prayers or energies. His touch can make everything flourish.

God is not deterred by our ordinariness

Even if, for one reason or another, we are not able to engage in high profile activity, there are other ways in which God can and will use our experience. Sometimes we claim, and that with much justification, that we are just ordinary people. By that we mean life's larger, more significant tasks are beyond us. We forget that we, ordinary people, represent the vast majority of the world's population. God has made so many like us that he must have a very special place in his heart for us! But there is a positive aspect to our ordinariness: we link best with those who are most like us and we who are ordinary provide a link, therefore, with the vast majority of people. Our faith, prayer and thoughtful service can speak volumes on behalf of our Lord.

God does not waste our sensitivity
On a specifically spiritual level, God has a commitment to making us more like his Son and in gentle ways he is always trying to draw us nearer to himself. In times of prosperity and self-sufficiency we tend to keep him at a respectful distance. However, when we are plunged into the troubled waters of bereavement) and know that we are hopelessly out of our depth, we turn to him

for deliverance and discover he does not fail us. Again, God uses our feelings of inadequacy and despair to forge new bonds with himself. He whose Son promised to share his peace and joy with us, and who was known also as a Man of Sorrows, is willing that we should share the profound consolations of his own heart. By so doing, he gives us practical comforts and resources that are far beyond our expectations.

God does not want to waste our future days

We have the rest of our lives to live. What we allow ourselves to become is as crucial for the present time as it is for eternity. The choice is ours, whether we go into our future largely disabled by the great loss we have sustained, or go forward, feeling impoverished by our loss, but enriched by the compensating grace of God. Death and bereavement are experiences for which we have little enthusiasm but, in reality, they are among the means whereby God's purposes for us are fulfilled. The bereavement journey must be one of life's hardest but, with Heaven as the goal, it is one of the most worthwhile.

All that my soul can need, this new day holds:
The grace to trust and, trusting, to endure;
The grace to know God's love my life enfolds;
The grace to prove his promises are sure.

INDEX OF TITLES

INDEX OF FIRST LINES